No better place than here

No better place than here

Dean Schabner

poems

atmosphere press

Contents

for Yiru
who gave me these poems

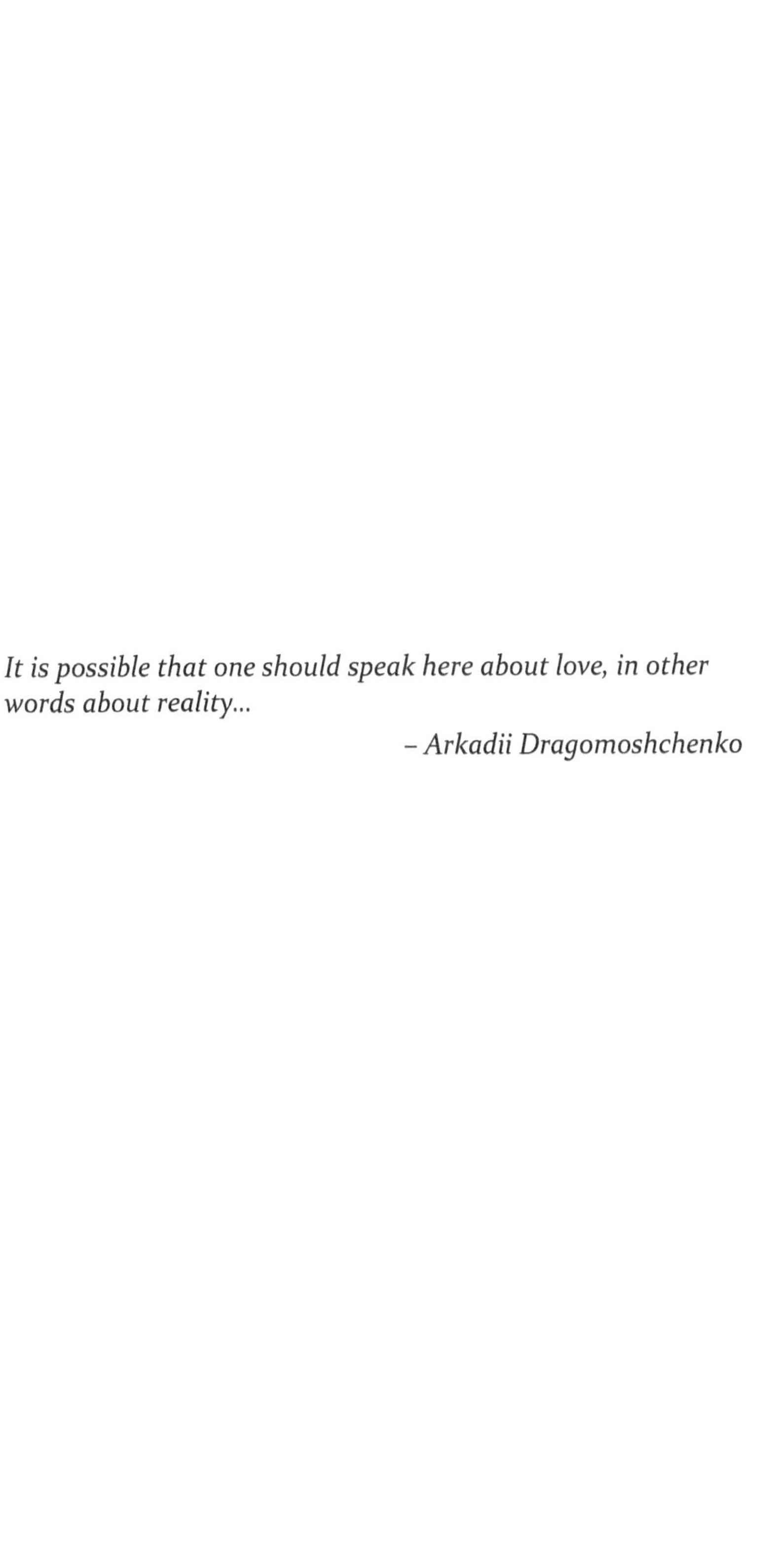

It is possible that one should speak here about love, in other words about reality...

– Arkadii Dragomoshchenko

windows open, breeze carried the whispering bay into my sleep
all night. then in the morning, I saw in the wetland this great
egret I seemed to know

> among the rushes
> head rising on neck erect
> firm long yet supple
> to rise into fresh morning
> to plunge — an egret — into you

*beside the house a pond fed by rains, by flood tides, where
long-legged waders feed*

    not one great egret
    came this morning to the marsh pond
    but three white and tall
    each might rather be alone
    such grace   I'd turn none away

waking again in the summer night, the salt air, I felt the
ocean, and someone who wasn't there.

    in bed it seems waves
    from the ocean rise silent
    drawing me to ride
    as all day I felt their pull
    another ocean calls me now

    waves it seems rise here
    winglike as if the ocean
    to ride not fearing
    their power their swell as when
    another ocean rises

Watching out the window as I should have been dressing, I saw a yellow crested night heron as if in contemplation on a rock by the water as the afternoon sun started to set.

has he forgotten
night heron at the bay's edge
he should be stalking
caught in his contemplation
I'm a frog awaiting his strike

by the water's edge
a night heron contemplates
forgetting to stalk
he gathers my scattered thoughts
drawn in unattached stillness

you've seen him now too
my night heron lost in thought
at the water's edge
contemplation unexpected
I can't help thinking of you

light of the falling
evening rising from the bay
a lone night heron
appears   his wings make silence
even among shrieking gulls

last light blazes up
red over the darkening bay
a lone night heron
let blackness fall   stars blossom
it's his wings create the sky

unlike the evening
red blazing up in last pride
a lone night heron
flies silent over the bay
seeming too dark to be seen

with no way to turn
back the fall of evening
a lone night heron
already himself darkness
mystery   flies into it

bay and sky ablaze
against the coming blackness
a lone night heron
flies unhurried   unconcerned
everything changes with him

alone in the night
hearing birds' songs off the bay
all alone and still
in their songs someone's voice comes
tender — warm — throw off the sheet

all unexpected
out of stillness   of quiet
fallen with darkness
how is it so softly geese
fill night with their tender call

unexpected but
not sudden their soft calling
breath-of-bay rising
even night   quiet   falls still
to listen to their whisper

unseen in bay night
in their voices their gentle call
steadiness of wings
all patience   all tenderness
in air alive to hold them

and stillness breathing
in their calling their wingbeats
enfolding unseen
in feathered embrace all light
as night they let carry them

in patience in breath
their voices come and tender
effortless   slow-winged
hold as they pass everything
still   just to hear their calling

a bufflehead

How is it lying in the quiet
the room dark and still but for breath
yours — mine — slipping between dream
the deep and waking —
that breaking the surface
a dark little duck
whitecheeked
waveformed body
rises — feathers waterjeweled
lit as by sun by stars by moon
each alight she tosses her head back
and rises wings aflutter to webbed feet
beak moving joyful her song laughter
in the still room as she casts off
the gems that clutter her wings her tail
her little rounded breast — until
unencumbered by anything not her
she settles quiet into water and herself

O to be that dark bay swell
breathing tidewise in the quiet room
and let her dive in us deep as she will

*a dark body flies overhead, as though just out of reach, but for
her voice that softly, insistent, fills the evening sky*

    what she means   calling
    goose in flight over the bay
    I cannot begin
    to say   but still I listen
    moved as though on her broad wings

I woke from a dream and could not sleep again, so I wrote this poem

> let's walk together
> morning is bright with birdsong
> last autumn's leaves lie
> all dampened by our night's spring storm
> our steps will make almost no sound

the murmuring

Say the brants
blackheaded in the night and
among themselves on the bay
excited could they be —
how green everywhere
will not hold back
not hold still and their voices
deep as earth and dark as
deep as still as the night

Yes it must be — the brants
blackheaded the windows open
come carried on their own
quiet voices into the room
to the bed to darkwinged spread —
the night too still the blackness
Nothing but their own winged voices
moving not even the water

Blackheaded darkwinged
the brants — but how
Their voices
too dark and still as night —
in the bed here the murmuring
irresistible as the tides
the brants the night's own
breath or is it yours

alba

Who let him in
the sun
to fill the room with his bluster
I want none of his light

Birds we all know
sing best before dawn
in the deep night you keep
in your hair

the ocean of night
breathing through you
your laugh your play
your ceaseless rise and fall

It's not brazen sun moves the tides
I'll be the moon
patient and gentle
yet fearless in darkest night

Big Indian Wilderness

Let's not talk
about the blackness
of your hair
Only children
talk in wonder
of the dark's thrills
of owls in flight
skies full of stars
things unseen we only feel

We're grownups
aren't we

No
Just let it fall
the blackness
and in it
sing the owl
his four-note song
Sing his voice
back to him
that the stars
one by one
will gather too
Sing him his song
Softly
His voice
Sing him to rise
take wing from the woods
that there'll be no end
to the falling dark

Thinking of an anxious summer night nearly two years ago, I composed these lines

    not as a raccoon
    stealing pizza so boldly
    the kiss I wanted
    so badly could only be
    wanted if given   freely

just a pear

The pear you gave me
firm and green
seemed just picked
hardly ripe
but when alone
I held it
firm and green
I saw again your hand
offering

Emboldened
I bit in

Juice overflowed my lips
soaked my fingers

Walking with someone through the summer evening in the city, I heard blue jays it seemed no one else heard, and later hearing them again in my head, I composed these lines

    passing 69th street
    jays call   I hear them   wildness
    loose in the city
    and walking with you   a call
    even more wild sings in me

blue jay blue

as morning is something
that's not a thing
but a happening
going on
so is the blue of this jay
as she calls high in the cold
the bare tree that reaches black
dividing ever more slender
more delicate into that blue
that goes on endless
beyond

the blue of this jay
when she takes wing
released on her slashing cry
her blue then
in flight
brightened by her black
her collar her tail bars
white and black
deepens
not steel not pale not gray
defiant of cold
of bare branches
of weak winter sun
defiant and deeper
herself
in her very blue
deeper even
than the blue
beyond

*after a mockingbird came to my kitchen window for the
berries in the bush there.*

>you   gray bird came right
>to the glass to feed on the twigs
>in cold sun there quick
>yet still I thought to catch you
>and now too quick   you are gone

*sparrows one by one hopping past me in the early evening, one
stayed close by me, patient, interested, it seemed. returning
the bird's attention, I saw something in her I didn't see in the
others, and, happy, I wrote these verses.*

   so generous you
   pause with me giving me time
   to notice at last
   the yellow just by your eyes
   that small difference   everything

they weren't close, the loud shimmering black birds as the sun,
falling, filled the sky with all the colors that had been too shy
to show at noon. they weren't close, but o their blackness,
their length, their grace

    boat-tailed grackles fill
    the trees with buds of night
    sunlit as evening
    falls and songs everywhere rise
    the world we make together

*three birds — songbirds — how they each sing thoughts of
someone*

> wanting only this
> to be within you as a
> catbird   simple   gray
> fills the day from a treetop
> with songs endlessly new

> how one could be two
> and the same   a songbird light
> among the leaves   quick
> and deep rolling ocean too
> that with one I fly and dive

> a green-winged kinglet
> gleaning among goldenrod
> in gentle fall sun
> no need to be anything
> else   when you're perfectly you

redwing song

watching while waiting for the train
a redwing blackbird perched
atop the highest branch of a maple
rising beyond the station wall
how with each burst of trilling song
he offers against the gray the chill
the rain that seems again readying to fall
he half spreads his wings the red
dark and bright rising
his chest swelling
atop the tree whose green is a light
of her own under the heavy clouds

his song
since after all
the rain comes the train will come
its rumble its braking screech
will overwhelm the delicacy
of his voice
may be futile
but there are other ways
after all
of seeing things

that voice on the wing
how a quick sparrow could be
ever thought simply
a sparrow with such a song
sets my heart too into flight

how it all appears

brown and bare the bush
but no — look — the branches
tipped in bushy buds
no
look — not buds — but alive
      O — songbirds
sparrows
      brown
    blackthroated
feathers fluffed and filling
winter air with
    bright
        crisp
   song

why wonder then
      soaked in sparrowsong
of love
for something
        so small

sparrow-colored tea
poured again in our white cups
I can't help myself
your hand is a bird I hold
gentle as blue morning sky

*On a path to see someone on a summer night I passed a place
where in spring trees were heavy with flowers and I wrote
these lines*

>   weeks ago blossoms
>   fragrant all fell from the trees
>   leaving nothing but leaves
>   is it only memory if
>   their scent's alive in my heart

*lost in thoughtlessness at the sink, when a bit of yellow, soft
as cloud and bright as sun, fluttered among the leaves.*

washing dishes — look
yellow warbler just outside
watches unconcerned
open window between us —
in every moment love

common yellowthroat

A chip of sun
fallen
alights on a reed
catching the blade
sideways—
Wings flutter
her beak rubs quick twice
up and down against the shaft.
Her fat little body
a yellowgreen tear
hanging heavy from clutching claws
ready to fall.
Heavy?
No.
The reed sways
yellowgreen like her
and bright in the sun —
sways
but does not bend.

I can't look away
but that's nothing to her
and she's off
like that
into the reeds
gone
stolen by flickering wings
herself her own thief
carrying off the secret
that in her quickness
I didn't know I'd seen

the nest found

lying in the grass it seemed
at first nothing but a ball
of grass and birch bark white
somehow gathered collected rolled
together but of course such things
do they often happen without help
and this not happenstance but
a nest fallen woven with care with
if it's not bold to say love and hope
a nest for eggs for lives to begin
and grow and even such a one as this
delicate and soft and now lost
to all but me for what it still
may hold I will not let it go

*a late spring morning hurrying the last bit to work, and there
on the sidewalk, a shattered speckled shell*

at first the empty
egg broken on the pavement
seems the saddest sight
but it's just what's tossed aside
from a new winged life above

*Watching from my window as bay and sky were lost in fog, I
wrote these lines*

    spring fog gathered close
    nothing of night left behind
    but gray emptiness
    solid it seems — nothingness
    yet there unseen gulls still laugh

innocence
(two poems of plovers)

by day

it can't be the sun or at least
it doesn't seem so late and
low in the sky the light warm and gentle
even now the beach almost empty
people gone home and gulls gathered
hanging in the air little clouds
gray and black and white while
along the water's edge darting up and back
as the waves run darkening the sand
and baring the tiny clams
that tip up to dig themselves back in
but it's the birds I mean the little ones
that run there that must be
plovers but move too quick to see
whether Wilson's piping semipalmated
the waterlive subtlety the quickness
of their movement bodies become sand
even in this clear tender light
coalescing into feathers flesh
always just out of reach
drawing eye and heart and breath on
like the one I sent you in flight
sent you hoping
when all I knew
was wanting to know

it may be true that was what
we'd come for the blackness
opening the ocean licking up
the flat wet sand to our feet
white frothed while overhead starless
sky arched unseen and fell
to meet horizonless the black
water that with its white
tumbling breakers would have us
have us and when you caught
my hand I thought you felt it
too the dizziness of standing
on the very edge the water
licking away the sand from under
our feet the limitlessness
of the thick black water
and water the lure and yet
it wasn't that its blackness
its emptiness endless
would swallow us because
in the squeeze of your hand
was a light song come darting
that suddenly white breasted
over the waves caught me up
as all together in flight
they cut this way then that
to come quicklegged
to ground O plovers

open water

the mystery is that though being
open as the ocean under midday sun
in sky blue and open to gulls and terns
to fly on easy open wings open the water
to dive and swim and ride the waves
that ceaseless yet never repeating
rise and break and rise and break and rise
you remain an ocean in whose depths
diving ever deeper I keep finding myself

a bit of lightning from dark gray clouds low over the bay, the
shaft quick, the great white birds diving, no less bright, and
somehow too, the sight of them, thinking of someone, still hits
hard as this thunder

    gannets yesterday
    dove headlong into ocean
    today thunderstorms
    rile the turquoise bay   without
    you how would I see either

riding up rising
waterslope   you scoter know
just when to dive as
breaker tumbles over you
and when to ride it out

ocean water still
too cold for me to dive in
yet you scoter joy
it seems in each white breaker
rising and tumbling for you

excitement seeing
how you dip under each new
tumbling white wavecrest
wings opening to take flight
into depths only you know

reappearing you
rise an instant to shake off
seafoam excitement
wings quick head stretching on long
neck and ready for what's next

again rushing wave
comes tumbling atop swellrise
you spread your wings   lift
yourself to dive once more
ocean's breath and yours and mine

wave rises patient
in itself its strength   power
while you all feathers
wings and tail all at home there
ocean gentled in knowing

watching the cormorants fishing, I wrote these verses

        his feathers won't keep
        water off   yet he dives deep
        in relentless search
        surfacing   just head and neck
        leave the waves   I could be him

        so close cormorant
        never before her red face
        long crooked neck here
        when she dives why be saddened
        absence a gift of presence

great egret in doubt

could it be that even you
standing on the water's edge
the bay stretched flat still gray
in front of you your slender neck
reaching all the way to your head
long and narrow and yellow beak
all the way never once
losing grace stillness light
you watch the cormorant
swimming far out there
black as you are white
curved neck slender body
half-submerged and wish
that like her you too could dive

egret in frustration

It must have been easy the catch
once seen
The little one round and green
no match
for the sunray strike
of yellow beak
but what triumph
is it the capture accomplished
when small green and round the little one is too big
to be swallowed
too hard
to be broken

egret taking wing

Is it the effort floats the grace
Not like the muttering mallards
who share the marsh pool
with the white —
Them — they open their wings
open and beating they're gone
the water the morning left behind
But you — how your legs
flex — how you longnecked
draw arrowhead back
as though to strike —
how your wings open feathers
how spread all whiteness
white even in the brown
the water that would hold you fast —
All wings and legs — white
White altogether too white to be
as all together
all at once
yet slow
your legs push to straighten
your neck releases arrowhead
skyward as your wings
your white wings gather
the instant —
And slow — air — breath — vision —
yes even the seeing slow as your wings
slow stroke by stroke
against the songfilled air
lift you O to flight —
Your great effort — yes
slowed to visibility
that we should know
how it is
beauty's gained

windblown hippie-haired
the merganser bobs on waves
raised green whitecapped wild
by the north wind awaiting
his deep-diving love's return

two days the wind blew
lifting water to whitecaps
tearing at the trees
autumn is here but the leaves
are not yet ready to fall

that you should be so
excited seeing snow geese
far across the bay
they hold night under their wings
like love   seen only in flight

in the gray morning
sleet   seeing blackwinged snow geese
flock over the pond
grace of each and all as one
they carry my thoughts to you

how gently restless
ocean holds the cloud-white gull
wave-winged   one with all
and having been held like that
once   there's no other release

while the others run
there's one plover over and
over lets the ocean
catch him soak him looking for
more   I too know an ocean

starting to rise

starting to rise
the wading egret white
from opaque water

legs and neck — curl in
and wings half open
starting — to spring

then though — no
long black legs
straighten — stiffen —

wings again lay flat
and long neck reaches
relaxes —

is it the morning sun
or the sudden music
of a yellowthroat

alighting in the egret
that he should — stay
to listen

white egret

the whiteness
      the length and
            the sunlit

the yellow
      the nakedness
            in the sun

the egret
      that I would be
            could I be

the whiteness
      sun itself
            and such wings

all slow all
      slow as though
            unafraid to show

how moved by sun
      waves' whisper
            a songbird's voice

not the egret —
      me
            become naked myself

sway and sigh

to sway and sigh —
the white nakedness
of an egret rising
in sun —

Or a reed in a songbird's grasp
as she alights
               sways and sighs
to be hers

that a great egret
even this late in summer
wouldn't give up
his breeding plumage I dig
mine too I still wear for you

a lone great egret
in dawn calm after three days'
wind blew in autumn
slow   fluid   his neck straightens
rising under sun's first kiss

*a day so cold even the sun seemed ice and the bay water only
stirred from freezing by the restless, unsteady wind. I walked
the shore and saw a brant, oddly alone his rough, soft voice
the only warmth*

    a brant wheels without
    seeming to move   spiraling
    down from clear blue sky
    waves reach for him   their fluid
    solidity   acceptance

a least bittern flew in to the pond outside my window, and
then I wrote this poem

    slow wings tenderly
    let him settle on a rock
    brown as the marsh pond
    bright sun in his legs his face
    beauty he wears light like yours

first green heron

The most common
the book says
where there are
herons — yet shy
solitary
and no sign of why
so named — neck
thick and brown and growing
from dark melon body
(not green at all)
to bladebeak head
and goldringed eyes

Shy perhaps yet still
and calm
contemplative
as if — wondering
while swallows all around
dip and dive and rise
feathered joy — as if —
and dragonflies
sunlit —
What is it
when you turn your head
both eyes sunringed
what is it
you see

glossy ibis

legs dangling orange
          from a body
— not dangling but
          as if
                    reaching
                              stretching
from a body that won't
decide it seems between
brown and red and purple and
                    green
taking sunplay — the all of it
as wings start
                    curl
                         hold
to let legs reach
          almost to the water
but then slowly
               carelessly
they push away the air
          lifting and long
                    downcurved beak
                    turning looking until
again wings hold
release again as if
to become one
with the ibis there reflected
          but no
even it seems this marsh pond water
          too firm too settled too resolved
for a body of such
                         fluidity

did you know   the night
not quite come   egrets roosting
white as midday clouds
kingfisher circling circling
it was your wings I watched for

dusk falls and egrets
even in their whiteness not
bright enough to keep
shadows off the quiet pond
you take flight   wings feathered sun

waiting and thinking
how nothing could be enough
cold now   shivering
egrets roosted   herons too
and then you spread your pale wings

six egrets came each
alone to roost in the trees
kingfisher circled
dark as the gathering night
only you raised wing against it

how you kept watching
as egrets came one by one
to rest for the night
did you know just when you'd catch
the day's last light in your wings

spring night

spring night comes in at the window
a house sparrow chirping inarticulate
could it be that sleeping wrapped
in this songbird season we smile
whisper and kiss into being makes
even the miracle of the turning year
something like superfluous

*the spring new moon has pulled the tide so strong, this
morning the bay seems all mud, sprouting tall waders and
darting sanderlings, plovers and sandpipers.*

> the bay tide's so low
> everywhere bottom's exposed
> no secrets   if I
> bared my heart this way would you
> like an egret come to feast

> why should I fear to
> bare myself like this tide gone
> out   the low water
> brings so many birds   sunlit
> the bay's a meadow in bloom

bufflehead again

Where water and air
meet in mutual caress
a dark little duck
swims dipping her head
in dark
in light
then quick as thought
she dives whole below

Long long she's gone
deep unseen
into the me unknown
'til suddenly
unchanged it seems
still small and dark
she breaks again the skin
where air and waves
paying no mind
play and dance
in kisses from the sun

She rises quick then
somehow finding footing
in shifting ceaseless wavelife
rises whitecheeked
head tossed back
spreads waterjeweled wings
from her little breast
opened now to the sun's delight
and she rises
rises
tossing aside
the unneeded jewels
she'd carried up
scattering them careless
from beating featherspring wings

Unneeded
when waves and sky
depths dark and light
all are hers
the diver
when even sun
is dizzied in the sky
to see her
small and dark and sure
risen but not to flight
wings beating just to shed
whatever isn't her
He dims his light in cloud
darkens the dancing bay
until she again encloses
her wavecurve breast
in dusky-feathered wings
and settles calm
back into water and herself

on seeing buffleheads this bright morning, how different from
yesterday under the heavy clouds

    in sunlight today
    the colors that in the gray
    hid in deep blackness
    shimmer live purple and green
    as I feel full of our love

    thinking of someone
    as buffleheads far from shore
    white among the waves
    dive   gone   and when seen again
    bright in sun from bay   reborn

    among the aimless
    uplifted little waves appear
    and disappear ducks
    diving and resurfacing
    constant   surprising   as love

winter rainbow

brightest by far
where it rises
fed from earth
from the
wetness
there fallen
all day and
half the night
before
as blooms
in months
to come
will be
joyous

only
as it rises
curving
as it does
reaching
over the dark
gray bay
it pales
seemingly
in distance
from its source
all the while
leaning
leaning
not wanting
perhaps
to leave us
until
rushing down
it regathers
as it falls
the bright force
of our desire

say
it won't last
can't last
nothing
lasts
but for now
there's enough
rain still
in the air
and sun
sun too
that together
look
it falls
bright
the miraculous
look
the real
look
there is no
better place
to see it from
than here

Acknowledgments

A portion of "innocence" appeared in the journal *Juniper*, in a slightly different form.

Thanks are due to the many people who have inspired me and taught me, by their words and by their way of living, in particular my mother and father, my brother, my lifelong friends Lynn and Barry, and of course my daughter, who has opened my eyes to how much magic there is in the world.

About Atmosphere Press

Atmosphere Press is an independent, full-service publisher for excellent books in all genres and for all audiences. Learn more about what we do at atmospherepress.com.

We encourage you to check out some of Atmosphere's latest releases, which are available at Amazon.com and via order from your local bookstore:

The Unsolvable Intrigue, poetry by D.C. Stoy

Words of a Feather Hawked Together, poetry by Linda Marie
    Hilton

Love, Air, poetry by Lawdenmarc Decamora

To Let Myself Go, poetry by Kimberly Olivera Lainez

less on that later, poetry by Madeline Farber

Granddaughter of Dust, poetry by Laura Williams

Nest of Stars, poetry by Nicole Verrone

Damaged, poetry by Crystal Wells

Aegis of Waves, poetry by Elder Gideon

Streetscapes, poetry by Martin Jon Porter

Feast, poetry by Alexandra Antonopoulos

River, Run! poetry by Caitlin Jackson

Etching the Ghost, poetry by Cathleen Cohen

Spindrift, poetry by Laurence W. Thomas

A Glorious Poetic Rage, poetry by Elmo Shade

Verses of Drought, poetry by Gregory Broadbent

Canine in the Promised Land, poetry by Philip J. Kowalski

Modern Constellations, poetry by Kendall Nichols

About the Author

Dean Schabner has broken fingers from playing basketball and a crooked nose from rugby. He grew up on the Great South Bay of Long Island and loved to climb trees. He's dug clams, framed houses, worked in all kinds of bookstores, and has been a journalist in Oregon, Mississippi, Boston, Connecticut, eastern Long Island, New York City, and Kyiv, Ukraine. He's a failed saxophone player who has yet to give up on the flute.

Dean lives on the shore of Jamaica Bay in the Rockaways of New York City. He has a chapbook of poems, *surf-body*, out from Ghost City Press and has had poems and stories appear in *The Trouvaille Review*, *Juniper*, *River Heron Review*, *Witness*, *Northwest Review*, Pushcart Prize and others. He's a body surfer who doesn't particularly mind if a wave takes him and tumbles him once in a while, and he's glad his daughter is that way, too.